PATTERN OF SCRIPTURE

CANTERBURY BOOKS

PATTERN
OF SCRIPTURE

by

Cecily Hastings

Father Vincent Rochford

Father Alexander Jones

SHEED AND WARD - NEW YORK

© Sheed & Ward, Inc., 1959

Library of Congress Catalog Card Number: 59–6397

Nihil Obstat: Rt. Rev. Matthew P. Stapleton, S.T.D., S.S.L.
                Diocesan Censor Deputatus

Imprimatur: ✠ Richard Cardinal Cushing
                Archbishop of Boston

November 21, 1958

Manufactured in the United States of America

Contents

God's Record of God's Work

CHAPTER I

God's Record of God's Work

The ordinary reading Catholic has very little knowledge of Scripture at all and practically none of the Old Testament, because he does not read it; or, if he does, his reading consists of short passages, dippings, and an endless re-commencement of the first chapters of Genesis. This is a rash generalization, founded on the insufficient evidence of casual observation, chiefly amongst newcomers to the Catholic Evidence Guild, and personal experience as an ordinary reading Catholic. The rest of this essay, concerned with the reasons for this situation and recommendations for remedying it, will be based entirely on one case, my own. Observation inclines me to think that others have much the same troubles; so, though I am aware that my factual starting-point

9

is inadequate, I shall go on from it nevertheless; anyone to whom my remarks do not apply at all will have to get help elsewhere.

We do not read the Scriptures. We cannot be bribed into it with indulgences, lured by new translations, or shamed by being assured, by St. Jerome and the Pope, that ignorance of the Scriptures is ignorance of Christ. I am assuming that there is no one reading this who is still under the impression that Scripture-reading, if not actually forbidden to Catholics, is nevertheless rather discouraged by the Church. I assume that we all know that it would be good to read the entire Bible. We do not read it. The reasons are, first, that it bores us; secondly, that it frightens, or at least worries us.

We may be conscious that part of the boredom arises out of the style of the Douai version, or any version closely resembling it. So the obvious remedy is to try something as different as possible: say, the Knox translation. We do this and find, to our dismay, that the boredom persists. We still get those same first chapters of Genesis read (the one part of the Old Testament which we do know, having tried this starting-again penance so frequently) and we still stick. If we struggle through Exodus, we still stick in Leviticus. The discovery that a fresh translation alone is not a sufficient remedy is apt to be discouraging. But it remains a reasonable and obvious rule to use for our Scripture reading whatever version we find most comfortable and attractive.

But we still have to overcome this primary failure to be interested by the Scriptures. It is of course possible to do some reading without any interest, by sheer will-power, and it is necessary to do it from time to time. But the Bible is a very large book: indeed, when printed as other books are it comes to several large books, and I think it would be very difficult to get through as much as that by will-power in the teeth of boredom.

There is one recommendation I should like to make at this point, merely on the same level as that of trying a new translation if the familiar one is unhelpful. It is to try a new starting-point. We make matters worse by always starting the Old Testament at Genesis I, 1, the New at Matthew I, 1. Try starting with a book you know you have never read: whether Judges, or I Kings, or Job, or Ezechiel, or Osee, the Epistle to the Hebrews, or Colossians, or the Apocalypse. At least that way some new ground will have been broken, some new light obtained by the time the often-repeated resolution dies once more.

The difficulty arising out of failure to be interested will, I believe, be more successfully met in the long run by attacking the other difficulty, that of fear. We are apt to be scared of the Bible, anxious lest it should prove too severe a trial to our faith to read much of it. Is it not true that we are repeatedly ready to rush to any new book of popular guidance to the Scriptures in a wild hope that at last this one really will provide comprehensive and totally satisfying solutions to all the difficulties that we have ever heard any rumour of concerning discrepancies between Genesis or Daniel on the one hand, say, and secular history on the other; mutually contradictory versions of events within Scripture (e.g. Kings v. Chronicles); all the bloody horrors discoverable in histories and psalms; Adam's rib, Noah's Ark, Jonah's Whale, the hare's cud, and the relationship of Joshua to the solar system?

I do not of course mean that we should not hasten to read such books. On the contrary, I could easily recommend a long list of them: above all the Atlas to the Bible produced by the Ecole Biblique at Jerusalem and published in English by

Nelson. It is more helpful than anything else, perhaps, in bringing the pages of Scripture to life,
bringing it home to us that these were real events
in a real, three-dimensional world. It is not by
any means merely an atlas, but contains commentaries on Biblical history as well. It gives help and
illumination in such a way as to dispel both the
boredom and the fear which, I have said, are our
two great obstacles to Bible reading.

There is a multitude of other books for the
ordinary reader which help in the same way. Many
difficulties can indeed be clarified and dispelled,
and the thread of a continuous, developing meaning for the Bible as a whole can be put into our
hands. But it is no good thinking that any such
book is simply going to demolish all those prob-
lems which we are vaguely conscious of as lying
in wait for us within the pages of God's book. No
guide or commentary whatever is going to leave
us able to say, of each in turn, "Well, that disposes
of *that*: nothing to puzzle over *there*." If we approach the Bible with the notion that somehow,
through more extensive information and the application of theories about literary genres and
copyist's errors, we are going to be able to reach
a point of comfortable reassurance, then we are

13

condemning ourselves in advance to get nothing out of the book but puzzles and even scandal. Moreover, the atmosphere of strain generated by our being permanently on our guard against the Scriptures while we are reading them will prevent us from enjoying them: the fear enhances the boredom.

Somehow, if we are to be successful in reading the Bible, we have got to enjoy it. So let us relax, sit back and enjoy it. Enjoy the high, poetic drama and the huge, awe-inspiring figures of Genesis, and forget for a while what we should be making of it all. Enjoy the poetry of the Psalms and the Song of Songs without bothering, for the time being, to wonder about their relationship to Christian morality and spirituality. Enjoy the dramatic narratives in the Books of Kings without worrying, just now, about our inability to like David, the preferred beloved of God as he was. If Judges seems more like a horror-comic than anything else, enjoy it as a horror-comic. If parts of Leviticus or Numbers strike us as more absurd than impressive, let us be content, for the time being, to be amused.

All this, it may be objected, seems to have very little to do with spiritual reading—and surely reading the Scriptures ought to be spiritual reading? I think that we make it almost impossible for ourselves to absorb the Bible as a whole if we think of it as "spiritual reading" in the sense of something immediately edifying. Of course, there are great tracts of Scripture—practically the whole of the New Testament, and a vast amount of the Old— which are indeed and obviously spiritually inspiring, and in which it is easy to sense the light and the food which we know we ought to be able to draw from God's word. But we shall only prepare unnecessary traps for ourselves if we insist on expecting to find this obvious edification everywhere. It just is not there. And if we avoid the difficulty by limiting ourselves to a sort of anthology of such portions of Scripture as we can easily feel are wonderful and impressive, then we deprive ourselves of the chance of growing into a sense of the Bible as a whole; and this is something we need.

Moreover, selective spiritual reading in Scripture is a positive encouragement to the scared feeling of which we must try to be cured. We must give up thinking of the Bible (I mean here especially the Old Testament) either as a fragile thing full of absurdities which must be somehow de-

fended against unbelievers lest it collapse altogether; or as a frightening, ferocious thing full of
hard sayings liable to damage our faith if we cannot hastily apply some adequate "explanation"
to the point of attack. God's written word is a
mighty reality superior to the cavillings of unbelievers, and not needing us for its defence. Nor is
it under any obligation to reassure us, to justify
itself at the bar of our criticisms and questionings.
Just as we ought, if we mean our faith at all, to
give up being nervous about Church history, for
the Church will never die because of the skeletons
in her cupboards, so we ought to give up being
nervous about the Bible: either defensive of it or
defensive against it.

We should be aiming, then, at familiarizing ourselves, by relaxed reading, unhampered by a
merely superficially reverential attitude, with the
Bible as a whole. We do not want to be subcon-
sciously thinking of the New Testament as a storehouse of texts and the Old as, more than anything else, a storehouse of difficulties. I have been
speaking mainly of the storehouse-of-difficulties
state of mind. Let us abandon equally the approach
to Scripture as a storehouse of texts, meaning
"proof-texts." How many quotations do we know

—isolated from their contexts, scarcely, if ever, even read in their contexts—which can be used as arguments for the papacy, the doctrine of one of the sacraments, the doctrine of purgatory, or some other point! Let us forget all about proofs, sometimes, and simply read the books as books—as biography, as history, as letters. And when we are studying dogma, let us make our own collections of passages. Let us, for instance, go all through the New Testament noting everything which seems to teach us directly about the doctrine of the Blessed Trinity, and watch the revealed truth growing organically from the pages of Scripture rather than seeing it diagrammatically laid out with selected texts marshalled in support. We should not, it is very true, have a hope of seeing it so grow out of our Scripture reading if we had not the clarifications of theology to tell us what to look for. But we need, with all due gratitude, to return from the text-book precisions to the richness of the Scriptural statement: and in the wholeness of its context, not dissected and classified.

As Father Rochford makes clear in his chapter in this book, we are on the wrong track altogether if we see the Scriptures primarily as a quarry for texts to illustrate an ordered, thesis-by-thesis exposition of dogma. For the Scriptures are the primary statement of dogmatic theology, God's own statement of it, which the ordered exposition can never be. If once we glimpse the vision of God's great plan, working its way through historical events, as recorded in the Scriptures, then our problem of boredom should be more than half overcome. But let us guard against thinking that from that moment all will be easy. We can make the same mistake over again at a more advanced level. He who approaches the Scriptures with a tidy text-book theology in mind, expecting to find nothing but illustrative texts for such a scheme, will be horribly shocked. But he who thinks that he is finally liberated from such a misunderstanding, who has glimpsed the great plan and approaches Scripture to contemplate its thrilling unfolding, can still receive some considerable jars. It is much easier and, at first, much more exciting, to read about the Exodus in some inspiring work of modern Scriptural theology than to read about it in the inspired words of Scripture. Exodus can seem a strangely clumsy, fumbling record of so overwhelming an event. And then, the reader knows, having driven his people out into the desert, God began his mighty education of them—

and we take a great mouthful of Leviticus and feel inclined to give up education for good.

For his vast purpose, he sent them into the Promised Land, to win it by the might of his arm and their own and to establish his kingdom of preparation there. We read in Joshua and Judges what that mighty act was like in terms of actual human events, of slaughter and destruction, and we begin to feel a little sick.

And so it goes on. On the one hand there is *our* vision of the great plan, on the other the tangled, often bloody, always rather messy muddle of concrete events. God's purposes were working through all the flesh-and-blood confusion of human history, not through abstract ideas. Somehow the marriage between the divine purpose and the human muddle has to take place in our minds. It cannot be done by straining the Bible to fit our preconceived pattern, even if it is no longer a pattern of dry, text-book theology. We have got to relax our grip and let the book be itself, whatever that may be. We have to stop minding whether it reassures us, edifies us: take it as it comes, without worrying so much about whether we can here and now solve the problem of how it all fits together; and certainly without cultivating the attitude that

19

someone, some expert popular-book writer, is under an obligation towards us to provide the answers.

We must, indeed, keep working away at all kinds of aspects of these apparent conflicts (not, I have suggested, restlessly, all the time; but nevertheless tirelessly, without ever simply giving the question up for good); feeling after possible resolutions and harmonies, following out all the lines of illuminating interpretation we are offered, working with helpful ideas and being ready to let them go when each in turn proves to be an over-simplification. (I assume that all who read this realize that none of this can be profitably done except within the limits of the Church's few authoritative interpretations.)

But whatever happens let us not be worried; for we know that this massive, bewildering literature is *as a matter of fact* God's record of God's work. *How* to discern the pattern in the weave may often be beyond us. But that it is there we know for certain; and every attempt to see it as a continuous whole, through whatever incidental tedious passages or startling puzzles we may meet, is rewarding beyond all proportion to our efforts.

The Plan of God

CHAPTER II

The Plan of God

Almighty God chose, out of his love, to make known to us men something of his nature and his purposes. He communicated to us knowledge we could get from no other source. What he revealed was not primarily any plan or design, it was himself; or rather, his presence among men. The manner in which he manifested himself was not through a series of truths or propositions, but through his action in history. By historical events occurring to one particular people throughout their formation and growth, by actions that should be signs and symbols pointing beyond themselves, by explanations and commentaries on the part of his prophets, he would show himself as present and active in the bosom of a definite racial group. So through his action men would come to understand his presence, through his presence derive some understanding of his designs, and finally something of his nature itself. And in the fullness of time he would become present to them in a new way, moving about amongst men as one of themselves, in Jesus Christ our Lord.

The written records of God's self-revelation have come down to us as the Bible. In fact this is less a book than a library. It contains seventy-three books written at different periods by many authors. Some were re-shaped and edited by other hands. The writers sprang from widely different backgrounds, social, economic and cultural. They comprise many literary modes—history, legend, allegory, poetry, aphorism. And all of them are Oriental in mentality, far away indeed from our Western technical culture.

From this mass of material how is a man to gain a clear view of his Maker, of his dealings with us, our destiny? What kind of friendship or union is possible between the transcendent God and himself? How can he hope to enter into it, and what demands does it make on him? How baffling these many books can be for the searcher! It is not to be wondered at that so many have closed their Bible in despair, retaining only a few isolated phrases they find inspiring; while on the other hand there is hardly any folly so extravagant that it will not claim the Bible for its justification.

THE BIBLE AND THEOLOGY

The human mind longs for definiteness and completeness in its knowledge; indeed, it is vital for man where his relationship with God is at stake. A man wants to believe; he must know what it is he believes.

The science which seeks to establish this certitude is theology. Because of its lofty subject-matter and the urgency of its task it is known as "Queen of the sciences." It must consider the great wealth of concepts, terms and images that Scripture and Tradition offer and must uncover with certainty the themes which God has made known, which men are bound to accept, which will colour their view of every human action and situation. It must arrive at precise formulations of divine truth, fixed certitudes which we call "dogmas." Exact technical terms are required for this, so that there may be no room for vagueness or ambiguity in its statements of belief. These dogmas must be set into proper relationship with each other, set out in logical order and in due proportion. Conclusions must be drawn from them which at any given moment may seem probably if not demonstrably true. Progress takes place, development occurs, her understanding of God and his designs grows deeper with the centuries. So, from material that is rich and vivid, yet to the individual mind confusing, Theology elaborates an organic intellectual construction which the mind can grasp and so come to apprehend something of God's majesty and wisdom and love. The construction of this comprehensive system of exact beliefs is the highest exercise of the human mind.

Therefore sacred Scripture is the foundation of dogma. And each dogma throws light on sacred Scripture. Each is necessary to the other. We have to move forward from the richness of the Bible to the precision of dogma; then, armed, safeguarded and enlightened by dogma, we return afresh to the Bible to gain deeper insight into the ways of God. Theology gives us a grip on what Scripture contains. It disengages for us the main themes and follows their unfolding in history. It prevents over-emphasis of some isolated elements at the expense of the whole picture.

Scripture demands the science of Theology. But Theology is not everything; it "belongs to sacred teaching," remarks Aquinas (*Summa,* I.l.i), but must not be used as a substitute for it.

Yet doesn't this happen, in practice? To listen to many a sermon, to read through a catechism, might easily give the impression that what God had revealed to us was Theology. . . . In explaining our faith we have had to concentrate for centuries on an apologetic presentation. We had to emphasize doctrines under attack from the Reformers. We were (and no wonder) frightened of a widespread dissemination of a book so complicated. We had to stress the organizational side of the Church, its hierarchical structure, its visible marks; all this was necessary during the long years of the great debate.

That debate is ended now, through the death of one of the parties to it. The typical Englishman of today is totally uninstructed in any form of Christian religion. Dislike of Catholicism, fear and suspicion of the Church, is a mood he inherits. But his difficulties are not those of the Protestant; they are the difficulties of the natural man, the good-natured materialist, the sinner. He needs feeding with God's revealing of himself, through the Bible.

27

That will appeal not only to the intellect, but to sensibilities, to emotive factors, to the subconscious, in a word to the whole man.

No understanding of Scripture can exist without the definitions, the theses and tracts of theology. But it is not through a technical vocabulary or the expert's divisions of thought that the Faith must be introduced to the masses. They must be offered a comprehensive view of God's working, the gradual unfolding of the divine plan; everything must be seen in relation to the economy of salvation. How many children leave school with several hundred catechism answers committed to memory, but never having seen the wood of the Faith for all the trees? Yet in fact everything that ever happened subserved the divine master-plan, what St. Paul calls "the hidden purpose of his will" (Eph. 1.10). He sees himself and his fellow-apostles as "publishing to the world the plan of this mystery, kept hidden from the beginning of time in the all-creating mind of God" (Eph. 3.9); it was "the secret hidden from all the ages and generations of the past . . ." but now God wills "to make known the manifold splendour of this secret among the Gentiles" (Col. 1.26–27).

THE CHURCH

Much of our apologetic in the last century pointed to the unrivalled coherence of the Catholic system as a strong argument in its favour. This is true, of course. But it is unlikely to carry great weight with a generation jaded with systems and theories. In our lifetime we have seen so many political and economic theories, and at least two international systems, proposed as panaceas, only to be exploded after brief periods of popularity. In consequence men today ask above all for facts. They have not sprung from generations nurtured on faith, they feel ill at ease with abstractions and universals. Looking for facts, they must be given God's "facts," his wonderful deeds, the "*mirabilia Dei.*" It is his "secret," his "mystery," working itself out in all its depth and range, that our post-Christian crowds need to hear; and this means all that God has ever done, all he is doing now, and all he will ever do throughout the whole course of history to bring about the salvation of the world.

And this means the Church.

The Church is not part of God's plan: it *is* his plan.

God's intention in creating was to unite to himself beings who should be worthy of his love. Following the shattering by man's sin of his original plan, he set to work fashioning a new one from the remnants of the old. The Old Testament is the record of that long, slow process; of God's patient pedagogy, always respectful of his creatures' liberty, moulding a selected part of humanity to his ends, as a potter slowly brings form and beauty into his crude clay, until it reproduces the image that was in his mind before he set his hand to his material. So our salvation is a matter of history, the story of God's forming for himself a people, of progress and set-back, with God making use of both, all culminating in the gathering together of men in Christ—that is, the Church. This is "the hidden purpose of his will" mentioned by St. Paul. "It was his loving design, centred in Christ, to give history its fulfilment by resuming everything in him, all that is in heaven, all that is on earth, summed up in him" (Eph. 1.9–10). In the divine mind Christ is the only-begotten and the first-born; in a sense God begets nothing but Christ. It is in him that God sees everything. God willed the Church from all eternity, willed it and contemplated it in his Word, his Son, just as it is in him that he sees and loves the world. But he loves the world for the sake of the Church. The Church was the latest act of his saving plan that God put into operation, but in his mind and intention it came first.

GOD CHOOSES FOR HIMSELF A MAN . . .

The Bible loses little time in coming to the earliest chapters of God's saving plan. It gives us the noble poem of creation; dramatically it allegorizes the rebellion of the first human pair; and at once shows the consequences of that act—sin, division, murder, oppression, cruelty; then the startling lesson of sin's punishment is taught in the legend of the flood.

So, rapidly, the stage is set, and we are prepared to witness God's first great intervention in our world with a view to founding his Church.

Somewhere near 1800 B.C. he communicated himself to a pagan named Abram; made himself known to him as the true God, and asked of him a great act of faith. This was to abandon the culture and comfort of his city, and follow God's beckoning into the desert towards the lands of the setting sun. There, in a land that God would show him, free from the contamination of an idolatrous society, he would learn to worship the true God, and would found a new clan. Abram's response to that call was to trust his God; he left home and was guided to the land of Chanaan. There his formation took place through years of hoping against hope for his heart's desire, a son. Puzzled, bewildered, he continued to trust and obey, whether in light or dark. Eventually his son Isaac was born; yet his sternest test was waiting for him, for before the lad had reached manhood God asked that he be slain by his father in sacrifice. Only at the last moment was Abram's hand stayed. So had he deserved his new name of Abraham, "father of many peoples," numerous as the stars or as the sands. But above all it would be through his posterity that all the nations of the earth would inherit a blessing.

Such was the man, stern monotheist among his polytheist contemporaries, man of rugged faith, who was to be the ancestor of God's people, both by blood and by faith.

The promises made to Abraham were renewed to his son and grandson. In the pages of the Old

Testament God is the God of Abraham, Isaac and Jacob, his promises to their ancestor the treasured heirloom of his descendants. We shall see how fully, if unexpectedly, those promises were to be fulfilled.

. . . AND A PEOPLE

In the course of time, Abraham's descendants, attracted by Egypt's welfare state, emigrated to that country. There they settled down and flourished, increasing rapidly in numbers and prosperity. When a new dynasty came to Egypt's throne it saw in this Semitic enclave a military weakness: up there on the North-Eastern border, sharing a common blood with potentially hostile neighbours, might it not provide a quisling element in case of war? It formed a grave menace; and in the interests of national security Draconian measures were employed. Their goods were confiscated by royal decree; they might not engage in commerce; education, administrative posts were denied to them; instead, they were formed into a servile labour-force for employment on public works or agriculture. When even this policy of repression failed to reduce their numbers, a policy of genocide was launched: the male infants of these Hebrews should be decimated. So, oppressed and despised, slaves in a foreign land, without confidence or hope, their fortunes were at the lowest ebb. The promises made to Abraham, transmitted to them by their fathers, were now dimmed and in imminent danger of being forgotten.

Yet it was from this material that God was to fashion himself a People of his own: and this was the moment.

But first it would be necessary to win their liberation. For this task God gave them one of the greatest leaders the world has seen, a man of Egyptian education but of their own blood. Whilst this man, Moses, was on the run because of a fatal blow struck in defence of his people, God revealed himself to him, communicated his very Name to him, Yahweh, "He-who-Is," and charged him to beard the proud Pharao and demand his race's freedom.

God intervened; a series of natural catastrophes weakened the king's resolve not to lose so valuable a pool of labour; and in one single day the whole muster of the people found themselves beyond the oppressor's power, on the far side of the Red Sea, on the verge of the desert.

Now, their liberation accomplished, a whole generation must pass its life in the desert; they need time to forget the lure of Egypt, the prestige of her gods, the influence of her wealth and culture. Alone by themselves, with Moses as their leader, with a constitution to live by, they must spend a whole lifetime in their novitiate. At the end the disparate rabble will emerge as a homogeneous, exclusive, proud people; the People of God.

They were given three months to adapt themselves to a nomadic desert life. Then Moses came down from the mountain where he had spent forty days in retreat, and in God's name offered them an Alliance. "I, to whom all the earth belongs, will single you out among its people to be my own. You shall serve me as a royal priesthood, as a consecrated nation" (Exod. 19.5). They, on their side, must recognize Yahweh and him alone for God. "I, the Lord, am thy God: I, who rescued thee from the land of Egypt, where thou didst dwell in slavery; thou shalt not defy me by making other gods thy own" (Exod. 20.1–2). Many other demands accompanied God's offer to them; at the

35

end "the whole people answered with one voice, 'We will do all that the Lord has bidden us'" (Exod. 24.3). So was made the first Covenant or Testament, offered in love and freely accepted. Abraham's descendants were now a people: they were adult.

They could now be taught something of the true God. They must learn that he is one; that he is a spirit; indeed, a person with a name of his own, Yahweh; and that he is holy, that is, separated, totally other.

The God of Sinai is not only a mountain-god; he is everywhere, all-seeing, all-directing; in the lightning, but also in men's hearts. The Covenant he had made with them was written down on stone tablets, as a visible sign that it remained in their hearts. They must pay Yahweh their worship through definite rites; but these must proclaim dispositions deep in their hearts. God is Israel's spouse, he has pledged himself to them, he is ever ready to forgive their infidelities; but lest their defection become absolute it will often be nothing save suffering that can keep them close to him.

Under the new legislation which enshrines the Alliance, destined to last till Christ should come and perfect it, their future lies open before them.

Surrounded by primitive barbaric tribes or by societies of high wealth and culture, it is they who were God's own Chosen People, repository of his revelation and vehicle for his saving plan.

Still they need territory of their own, and it is earmarked for them, a land that will seem to them, in comparison with the desert, one flowing with milk and honey. But it will not be theirs without a struggle. They will have to fight both for their soil and for their soul. Small wonder, then, that they were fiercely nationalistic; they had to be, in order to protect their existence, and therefore the survival of the religion committed to them. And their national pride would prevent them from falling into a merely individualistic conception of salvation. Individuals were to be saved through their membership of the People.

In the desert at the mountain's foot this mob of bedouins, called by God to be his own and bound to him in Alliance, start their long, chequered yet glorious march through history: the one people of all humanity to be standard-bearers of monotheism in a world given to worship of repulsive, cruel idols. This was their vocation; and powerless and insignificant as they seemed, Yahweh would be their champion.

GOD'S PEOPLE NEEDS A HOME . . .

During a lifetime spent as nomads, stained by many moments of infidelity to Yahweh, they were on their way towards a land flowing with milk and honey: Palestine. Like so many of God's gifts (including salvation itself), it still had to be conquered. This was the work of a hundred and fifty years. Their new leader, Josue, apportioned the land out among the twelve tribes; but the Chanaanite inhabitants had to be expropriated and tamed. These were years of continuous warfare against inhabitants or external enemies. Years of temptation, too; for in turning from a nomad existence to the stable life of farmers, they had to learn from the Chanaanites; and among other things they learned about Baal, the false god who would never remain very far from their horizons. Only when Yahweh withdrew his protection and they knew military defeats, did they realize their faithlessness and return to their God. Slowly they completed the occupation of the Promised Land, ruled by Judges, by Jephte, Gideon, Samuel.

Like children, they came to tire of their leadership; why shouldn't they have hereditary rulers, like their neighbours? "Give us a king, such as other nations have" (1 Kings 8.5), they said to Samuel; and full of forebodings, he anointed their first king, Saul, and the theocracy became a nation. Saul inaugurated a century of prosperity and expansion; but himself soon proved faithless, and was succeeded by the shepherd lad David, the ideal ruler, King after God's own heart, from whom the Messias was to be descended. He was able to give his people security and peace, conditions of prosperity. He founded their political and religious capital, Jerusalem, and brought thither the Ark of the Covenant, and the Tables of the Law. He organized their liturgy—we are still using much of it.

His son, Solomon, was able to carry out his father's dream of a majestic temple in Jerusalem which should speak of Yahweh's grandeur to his People. For this he was able to draw on the richest materials the Middle East provided, some acquired by commerce, others as tribute. Yet his story is tragic, for he lapsed into paganism, and the Jewish monarchy from that day in 935 B.C. failed to provide more than a couple of kings who understood their responsibilities as divinely appointed rulers of a divinely chosen people.

. . . AND AN IDEAL

For the next four hundred years the tale is one of prosperity, of Yahweh half-forgotten, of acceptance by rulers and masses of Baal and other pagan gods. Yet a succession of men inspired by Yahweh to speak in his name proclaimed unceasingly the Alliance to which the Chosen Race was being unfaithful. The God of Sinai was not slumbering! His holiness, his infinite might and his jealousy would strike them for their own good! The prophets— Elias, Isaias, Jeremias and Ezechiel and their like —denounced idolatry both by word and action; social injustice, oppression of the poor by the rich; empty formalism of worship, where holy actions no longer corresponded with dispositions of heart.

At the same time they preached a more spiritual conception of religion than the people had held hitherto. Outward conformity with a code was not holiness, Yahweh demanded moral virtue; sin is opposed to sanctity, it brings separation from God. Yahweh's commands were dictated by his love for his People, their faithlessness had not forfeited his love.

After Solomon's death, his country was divided

into two kingdoms. The Northern one, Israel, was not to enjoy more than a century of independence; Juda, on the other hand, survived, often precariously, for three hundred and fifty years. Threatened by powerful neighbours, feverishly seeking political alliances when in fact, as the prophets urged, the only dependable one was the Alliance of Sinai, their need of rescue and safety became their constant preoccupation. This salvation would come, repeated the prophets, from Yahweh. He was still their shepherd. He would establish amongst them a new kingdom, its leader the Messias who should come. But if they placed their confidence elsewhere than in Yahweh, they would suffer terrible retribution, for he would abandon them to the power of their enemies. The lesson was not taken to heart, and in 586 B.C. Jerusalem fell to the armies of Babylon. It was sacked and utterly destroyed. All the leading classes of society and many workers and peasants were deported in long, mourning caravans, to an exile that was to last a lifetime.

Once again deported slave-workers, once again strangers in a pagan land, their temple and its worship only a memory, they were in danger of compromise. Some settled down to make the best of it and flourished—the Babylonian treasury was glad to borrow large sums from Jewish finance-houses. By reaction a minority, grouped round the prophet Ezechiel, turned more and more to their religion. "By the rivers of Babylon, there we sat and wept, remembering Sion . . . If I forget you, Jerusalem, may my right hand wither!" they repeated. (Ps. 136.1,5.) The "faithful remnant," the *anawim,* the Poor of Yahweh, learned their faith anew in suffering, and developed more of its implications. When Cyrus of Persia overthrew the power of Babylon and signed an order for the return of the captives, in 535 B.C., a powerful body among God's Chosen People had learned the lessons of their history, so that they carried back to their ancestral home not only bitter memories but a true social ideal.

A GENUINE RELIGIOUS COMMUNITY

With what exaltation of heart the exiles set foot again on the ruins of Jerusalem, setting about the task of raising again an altar and temple to Yahweh! Sharing deeply in a commonly held ideal, they had a burning desire to understand the prophets, the Covenant and the Law. In these years the true Jewish soul was born. Sacrifices they would offer again—but the best of sacrifices is a bruised heart, for at least the Poor of Yahweh recognized their sinfulness. The new faith in the Holy One of Israel was even to produce martyrs like Eleazar and the Machabees. Beyond Israel of the flesh they begin to glimpse a spiritual Israel, overlapping race. Through their love of Jerusalem and its glory they dimly saw a spiritual Jerusalem in which converted heathen nations would adore the true God.

There was immense hope that "He who is to come" would not long delay; he would be "Son of David," with investiture from heaven. One of Isaias' disciples wrote "Ah, if Thou woulds't tear the heavens apart and come down!" When he came he would establish a new covenant or alliance suited to the new messianic era and surpassing the old Covenant of Sinai. How strongly all this current flows through the Qumran literature!

Their racial nationalism began to yield to a spiritual universalism. The whole earth was to benefit from the Promise made to Abraham. "There be nations a-many that shall rally . . . to the Lord's side; they, too, shall be people of mine"

(Zach. 2.11). It would be their honour to be God's apostles: "They shall go out where men never heard of my name, never saw my glory yet, to reveal that glory among the nations," Isaias' school foresaw (Is. 66.19).

Meanwhile they experienced for another four centuries the rule of successive alien masters. Then, beginning in 143 B.C., they enjoyed eighty years of independence, only to be occupied by the Roman legions under Pompey and incorporated into the Empire. It was inevitable that whilst they retained a fierce nationalistic pride and religious fervour, they should more and more widely interpret liberation, salvation, kingdom of the Messias in political terms. "Peace this king shall impose on the world, reigning from sea to sea" Zacharias had promised (9.10): longing for independence, ready for rebellion but riddled with collaborators, they came to assume that the Saviour would turn the tables, overthrow proud Rome, and found a Jewish empire that would last for ever.

Such a conception prepared them all too well for the great tragedy of their history: their failure to recognize the Saviour whose coming they alone foreknew. As a people, they failed; yet the faithful remnant knew from the beginning. His Mother praised God, before he was born, for remembering "the promise which he made to our forefathers, Abraham and his posterity . . ." (Luke 1.54). The priest, Zachary, realized that Yahweh was fulfilling the "oath he had sworn to our father Abraham" (Luke 1.73). The devout old man Simeon, the pious woman Anna, recognized him and talked of him in their own circles, to "all that patiently waited for the deliverance of Israel" (Luke 2.38).

This strange race, unique in history because they filled a unique role, had fulfilled their destiny. Chosen as witnesses to monotheism, in order that among pagans and idolaters they at least should pay worship to the true God, and to prepare the way for the coming of Jesus Christ; their whole history dominated by the covenant and alliance Yahweh had made with them at the foot of Sinai; sinful, often unfaithful, narrow and arrogant; nevertheless they had, in substance, fulfilled their mission. Looking back, they had never quite forgotten God's intervention to set them free from Egyptian oppression; looking forward, they had never quite lost their hope in Christ to come.

Thus the first long chapter of history was over. Now, God could start to write the second.

A second which would continue the first, carrying on the same story at a higher level.

Christ our Lord said he had come not to "set aside the law and the prophets . . . but to bring them to perfection" (Matt. 5.17). In fact many of the persons, events and institutions of the Old Testament derived their chief importance from the fact that they pointed beyond themselves towards the great realities of the New Testament, and indeed prepared the way for them. The Chosen Race, bound by covenant to God, living under his law, praising him through the ages for setting them free from slavery in Egypt, looking forward to the coming of Christ on the earth—all these were "prophetic" in St. Paul's word (1 Cor. 10.3); or "mysteries," to employ a favourite word of the early Fathers; moments in the working out of God's plan; or, again, "types," to use a more modern expression.

They were embryonic, for they were signs pointing to more real elements of God's plan, but also initial stages in men's progress towards them. They contained in themselves higher realities and at the same time developed in the course of providence into those realities. They were symbols whose fulfilment far surpassed them, yet was imminent in them. The Chosen Race, an earthly people, was but the symbol of a new Chosen Race, a supernatural people of the redeemed; but it prepared the latter's coming into existence. The old Covenant, Testament, was but a shadow of the "new, everlasting Testament." The old Law of the decalogue, with its manifold prescriptions, was only a figure of the great new law of charity. The spirit of thanksgiving for emancipation from Egypt was to find a superior fulfilment in the thanksgiving of the new People for its liberation from the shackles of sin and death; the very Sacrifice of the New Law was to originate within the framework of the Passover meal, to make it real by our offering to God and then sharing in the true Paschal Lamb. And the expectation of Christ's redemptive coming was to blossom into anticipation by the redeemed of the coming of their Saviour in glory.

And all this means the Church!

For the Qahal Yahweh, the assembly of the Chosen People summoned by God, burdened as it was, in spite of the prophets, with racist ambitions and temporal hopes, was the Church-before-the-Church. Indeed, the translators of the Septuagint called it "the Church of God." The authentic founder of the Catholic Church was none other than Abraham himself. Israel was prophetic, a "mystery" in the sense given above; an earthly sign pointing beyond itself to the eternal Church, and preparing for its coming.

HOW THE APOSTLES THOUGHT OF THE CHURCH

In the Old Testament the Chosen People had been God's flock of sheep (Ezech. 34; Jer. 10.21, 13.20, 23.1–4, 25.34; Zach.; Psalms). Our Lord had several times spoken of his flock. What more natural than that St. Paul, talking to the clergy of Ephesus, should speak of "God's Church . . . that flock which he won for himself at the price of his own blood"? (Acts 20.28).

"Greetings to the church of God at Corinth, to those who have been sanctified in Christ Jesus, and called to be holy" (I Cor. 1.2). The word "church" (*ekklesia*) might mean the local community or the universal, but always it meant those who had been "called" (*kaleo*), and like the Hebrew *qahal*, emphasized God's initiative in choosing who should be called to membership and freely giving them the grace. The word bore no reference to numbers, it signified the totality of God's people, a reality greater than any numerical manifestation.

Vivid as these phrases were to the Jewish mentality, the idea they conveyed was stated explicitly when St. Paul wrote (Gal. 6.16) of "God's *true* Israel."

Yahweh had promised the Israelites in the desert: "I . . . will single you out among the peoples of the earth to be my own. You shall serve me as a royal priesthood, as a consecrated nation" (Exod. 19.6). Now St. Peter tells his audience "You are a chosen race, a royal priesthood, a consecrated nation, a people God means to have for himself. . . . Time was when you were not a people at all, now you are God's people" (1 Pet. 2.9). And St. John was to echo this in his Apocalypse (1.5–6): "Jesus Christ . . . has made us a royal race of priests, to serve God, his Father."

The new flock, the new *qahal,* the new Israel, the new Chosen Race sprung from and perfecting the old! Bound to God by a new Alliance or Covenant as the old had been, but this time one that should never pass away. Moses, accepting the Hebrews' ratification of the old testament, had sprinkled the people with the blood of the sacri-

ficed bullocks, saying: "Here is the blood of the
covenant which the Lord makes with you" (Exod.
24.8). It was in words similar, yet infinitely trans-
cending them in meaning, that our Saviour inaugurated the new Covenant: "This cup is the
new testament, in my blood" (1 Cor. 11.25). And
this new Covenant must express itself in a law, as
the former one had: in the new law of charity:
"God . . . has enabled us to promulgate his new
law to men" (2 Cor. 3.6).

The old Israel was God's kingdom: the new
Israel, the Church, is "Christ's kingdom, God's
kingdom" (Eph. 5.5). The prophets had likened
it to a field or a temple of which God is the archi-
tect. So St. Paul writes to his converts: "You are a
field of God's tilling, a structure of God's design"
(1 Cor. 3.9). "You too must be built up on him,
stones that live and breathe, into a spiritual fabric,"
says St. Peter (1 Pet. 2.5). "The foundation which
has been laid is the only one . . . Jesus Christ"
(1 Cor. 3.11); "the chief corner-stone . . . is
Jesus Christ himself; in him, the whole fabric is
bound together, as it grows into a temple, dedi-
cated to the Lord" (Eph. 2.21): indeed, even
their "bodies are shrines of the Holy Spirit" (1
Cor. 6.19).

The metaphors in which the Scriptures described the first People of God came naturally to the apostles' minds as they set about explaining the New People: no mere society of individuals but a spiritual people into which a man must be incorporated if he is to be saved. So it was that Gentile converts came quite naturally to speak of the Jewish patriarchs as "our fathers, our ancestors." So today we pray during the Easter vigil: "Grant that the whole world may become children of Abraham and enter into the heritage of Israel."

SPOUSE OF CHRIST

God had spoken of Israel's relationship with him as that of a wife. "Everlastingly I will betroth thee to myself," he had said through his prophet Osee (2.21). Unfaithfulness on her part towards him was a spiritual adultery. "A wanton land . . . that keeps troth with its Lord never" (Osee 1.2); "Fatal beauty . . . emboldened thee to play the harlot" (Ezech. 16.15); "thou with many lovers hast played the wanton" (Jer. 3.1).

The new Israel, then, *is* Christ's spouse. Husband and wife are the complement, each to the other; and this relationship is the outward sign of Christ and the Church, complementing each other in unity, a unity in which they remain distinct, with the Church in a relationship of dependence and submission to Christ. "You who are husbands must show love to your wives, as Christ showed love to the Church when he gave himself up on its behalf. He would hallow it, purify it . . . he would summon it into his own presence, the Church in all its beauty, no stain, no wrinkle, no such disfigurement; it was to be holy, it was to be spotless." So writes St. Paul (Eph. 5.25–28). St. John, too, uses the same metaphor: "the new Jerusalem . . . all clothed in readiness, like a bride who has adorned herself to meet her husband . . . that bride, whose bridegroom is the Lamb" (Apoc. 21.2,9).

It is as spouse of Christ that the Church brings us to new birth, birth through water and the Holy Ghost, to be children of God. It is through his spouse and his mystical Body that Christ communicates himself. The Church begets them to him, and is their Mother. Comparing the new Jerusalem, the Church, with the old, St. Paul says "the heavenly Jerusalem is our mother" (Gal. 4.26). Chosen as apostle and sent to the Galatians by Christ's spouse, he seems to identify himself with her when he exclaims: "I am in travail over you afresh, until I can see Christ's image formed in you" (Gal. 4.19).

By her sacraments the Church bears us to the life of Christ and nourishes that life in us. By her teaching authority she shares in his. It is in virtue of her motherhood that she punishes us when we need it. And because she is our Mother, we obey her as sons, and love her in obeying.

Her union with Christ is therefore fruitful; and "no man can have God for his father who has not the Church for his mother," as Augustine said so long ago (*In Ps. 88*).

THE VINE

"It is the house of Israel that the Lord called his vineyard" (Is. 5.7). "Long ago, thou didst bring a vine out of Egypt, rooting out the heathen to plant it here; thou didst prepare the way for its spreading, and it took root where thou hadst planted it, filled the whole land . . . God of hosts, relent, look down from heaven, look to this vine, that needs thy care" (Ps. 79.9,15).

Our Lord himself took up the traditional phrase to illustrate our oneness of life with him. "I am the vine, you are its branches; if a man lives on in me, and I in him, then he will yield abundant fruit; separated from me, you have no power to do anything" (John 15.5–6). The community of God's people lies within them; it is a unity of life.

"I have planted, Apollo watered, but God gave the increase" (1 Cor. 3.6).

Keeping to the same figure of speech, but replacing vine with olive, Paul emphasizes (Rom. 11.17) how the Church of Christ grows out of Israel. "The branches have been thinned out, and thou, a wild olive, hast been grafted in among them; sharest, with them, the root and the richness of the true olive." Always, in the apostolic preaching, God's plan was one, its later developments continuing the beginnings on a higher plane of reality.

MYSTICAL BODY OF CHRIST

But St. Paul's deepest and most favoured term for the Church was "the body of Christ." So many centuries after, Pius XII says: "To define and describe the true Church of Jesus Christ—that Church which is holy, catholic, apostolic, Roman —no more beautiful, excellent, even divine expression can be found than that which terms it the mystical Body of Jesus Christ" (*Encycl. Myst. Corp.,* 13).

"We, though many in number, form one body in Christ," says the apostle (Rom. 12.5). "I am glad of my sufferings . . . for the sake of his body, the Church" (Col. 1.24).

During his lifetime on earth, God the Son was present in our world in the human body he had taken from Mary. It was through the eyes of that body that he saw, gave love and attracted men. Through its lips he taught them. With its hands he blessed them, cured them, embraced them and was nailed to the cross for them. On its feet he pursued men in search of their souls.

Now that body resides in glory in heaven.

But God the Son is still present and active in the world of men in a body; now, in a body taken from the womb of all humanity, a body composed of human beings united with him by sharing his life. That body is the means by which Christ is inserted into a world to be saved. Through it he continues to teach, to bless, to heal, to feed, and to suffer.

Humanity was predestined in Christ, and Christ was predestined corporately with all humanity. The mystery of salvation, which came into being in the man Christ Jesus, affects the whole human race. "A man's body is all one, though it has a number of different organs; and all this multitude of organs goes to make up one body: so it is with Christ" (1 Cor. 12.12). That is, Christ together with the redeemed form one mystical person, "the New Man" of St. Paul, or as St. Augustine was later to call it, "the total Christ."

Of this body Christ is the head. "He has put everything under his dominion, and made him the head to which the whole Church is joined, so that the Church is his body, the completion of him who everywhere and in all things is complete" (Eph. 1.22–23). "It was God's good pleasure to let all completeness dwell in him, and through him to win back all things, whether on earth or in heaven, into union with himself, making peace with them through his blood, shed on the cross" (Col. 1.19–21). On "Christ who is our head . . . all the body depends; it is organized and unified by each contact with the source which supplies it . . . and

56

achieves its natural growth, building itself up through charity" (Eph. 4.15,16).

From him comes an influx of divine life. "If . . . one man's fault brought death on a whole multitude, all the more lavish was God's grace, shown to a whole multitude, that free gift he made us in the grace brought by one man, Jesus Christ" (Rom. 5.15). The Son receives his life from the uncreated fullness of God; and it is from the Son's fullness in turn that the members of his body will have that life. Our life is his; there is no opposition between head and trunk; the union between him and us is the most intimate possible. This community of men with Christ is the mysterious essence of the Church. No wonder that Saul, who had heard on the road to Damascus: "Saul, Saul, why dost thou persecute me?" (Acts 9.4), learned that Christ and his members are one: "You are all one person in Jesus Christ" (Gal. 3.28); how often and how naturally the phrases come to his pen, we "in Christ Jesus" and "Christ in us." How well had Joan of Arc, the little country lass, grasped the same truth, shearing through the intricate subtleties of the professional Canon Lawyers with her "It's all one and the same, Jesus Christ and the Church!"

God's flock, God's people, new Israel, his Kingdom, Spouse of Christ: all these the Church is, fulfilling the Old Testament realities and bringing them to their perfection. But even more: branches of the Vine that is Christ; very body of Christ: the Church IS Christ.

THE PROMISES TO ABRAHAM FULFILLED

So at last the promises God made to Abraham are fulfilled. He was to have an heir, numerous descendants, and "all the races of the world shall find a blessing through thy posterity" (Gen. 22.18). But Isaac, his son, is only the figurative heir; his real heir was Jesus Christ: "the promises," St. Paul points out (Gal. 3.16), "were made to Abraham and his off-spring [singular]," not to his descendants. Abraham's heir was God the Son incarnate in the flesh; heir of God inasmuch as he was the Word of God; heir of Abraham according to the flesh. Does not St. Matthew begin his gospel with the words: "A record of the ancestry from which Jesus Christ, the son of David, son of Abraham, was born"? The figurative inheritance promised to Abraham was Chanaan; the real inheritance is the very life of God himself, given to us in Christ.

"In Christ Jesus, the blessing of Abraham was to be imparted to the Gentiles, so that we, through faith, might receive the promised gift of the Spirit" (Gal. 3.14). It is Christ, dead and risen again, who sends the Spirit and all God's riches: and it was to this that the promises referred.

And the beneficiary? Not the old Israel of the flesh, but the new, real Israel, the spiritual and universal Israel: the Church. The "posterity" of Abraham includes all who are united to his heir, Christ. "If you belong to Christ, then you are indeed Abraham's children: the promised inheritance is yours" (Gal. 3.29). Indeed, to claim merely physical descent from the patriarch is of no avail. "Do not think to say 'We have Abraham for our father,' " Christ warned the Jews; "if you are Abraham's true children, it is for you to follow Abraham's example" (Matt. 3.9; Luke 3.8; John 8.33–40); words amplified by St. Paul: "You must recognize, then, that Abraham's real children are the children of his faith" (Gal. 3.7). No longer was blood or rite of circumcision to count: the new, spiritual Israel sprung from Abraham would be universal, and truly, through our Lord and his Church, "all the nations of the earth shall be blessed." Abraham was the founding father of the Catholic Church.

THE NEW COVENANT

Yahweh had pledged his presence and protection to the children of Israel by means of a covenant, and Moses was his intermediary in proposing it to his people, as he was theirs in accepting it. Ratified with sacrificial blood, it was expressed in and safeguarded by the Mosaic Law.

With the coming of Christ, all this was to change, for the Old Testament was but figure of a New. "Do not think that I have come to set aside the law and the prophets; I have not come to set them aside but to bring them to perfection" (Matt. 5.17), he said. Figure was to yield to reality. Between the two would remain continuity—the continuity of transposition: old will have prepared the way for new, new will utterly transcend old.

Philip, hastening home after his first introduction to Jesus, told his brother "We have discovered who it was Moses wrote of in his law" (John 1.45); our Saviour, discussing the news with disciples on a country road, "going back to Moses . . . began to interpret the words used of himself by all the scriptures" (Luke 24.27); and Moses himself was present at the Transfiguration, witness, as it were, to his own fulfilment, for Christ was mediator between God and his New People, as Moses had been for the Old People, and established with them the New Covenant of which the Old had been no more than the figure.

How our Lord, as he institutes the New, embodying it in a sacrificial banquet as the Old was, and giving them "the uttermost proof of his love" (John 13.1)—"I have longed and longed to share this paschal meal with you before my passion" (Luke 22.15)—echoes the words of Moses as he inaugurates the new dispensation! For Moses, ratifying the Covenant or Testament of Yahweh at the foot of Sinai, had offered sacrifice of bullocks. He had poured out some of the blood on the altar; the rest he "took . . . and sprinkled it over the people, crying out: 'Here is the blood of the covenant which the Lord makes with you'" (Exod. 24.8). At this moment, when "the old is by the new replaced; the substance has the shadow chased" (*Lauda Sion*), the Saviour, one sole mediator between God and man, about to offer himself in sacrifice, uses the same form of words: "This cup is the new testament, in my blood" (1 Cor. 11.25)—the New Covenant that will never pass away, "new and everlasting testament."

Even the Greek word used for "new" is full of significance. " '*Kainos*' means 'new,' but there was another word in Greek which also meant 'new,' '*neos,*' familiar to us in expressions like 'neo-Thomism,' 'neo-cubist.' But the shade of difference between the two adjectives is very important. When the word '*neos*' is used, it means the substitution of one person or thing for another, like the new landlord: a different person altogether. On the contrary, the word '*kainos*' means simply the renewal of the same substance, the same reality."[1] The whole point we are making, namely that the New Testament, new law, new Israel are but the perfect developments of the old, is contained in that single word.

"I will give them their recompense, bind myself, now, by an eternal convenant," God had promised (Is. 61.8). How far superior the new one is, the Epistle to the Hebrews shows; for the mediator of the new is no longer God's servant, as Moses was, but his Son; the priest of the new covenant is perfect and sinless, the sacrifice he offered perfect and self-sufficing in its own right.

In the new Law which accompanies the new testament, Christ purges the old one of its deform-

[1] Yves Congar in "L'Etat d'Israel dans le dessein de Dieu," *Parole et Mission*, No. 2, p. 172.

ations. "They have sat in the chair of Moses . . . woe to them!" "Do not suppose that it will be for me to accuse you before my Father; your accusation will come from Moses, the very man in whom you put your trust" (John 5.45). No, the new law would not concern itself with ceremonial formalities or with minutiae. It was to be internal, it would be possible to offend against it by malice of mind, without ever lifting a finger to perform the malicious act: the man who is angry with his brother (Matt. 5.22), who lusts after a woman (Matt. 5.28), has already committed murder and adultery in his heart. It was a universal law, the law of love, of which Christ himself is the model: "your love for one another is to be like the love I have borne you" (John 13.34).

Indeed, Christ is both covenant and law. The new covenant binding God with man is a Person, the Person of Jesus Christ, in whom God and man are united for ever. And the love to be given would not even be our own; all we can do is to remove obstacles to Christ's action in us, so that it is less we loving our neighbour than Christ loving our neighbour through us. What a fulfilment and what a transposition here from the less real realities which foreshadowed the new dispensation of God!

THE KINGDOM OF GOD

The former Israel had been God's kingdom; he had acquired royal rights over the people by setting them free and making them into an independent nation. They formed "the Kingdom of God," a worldly kingdom in the world, but still God's.

And this was but the faintest foreshadowing of the true kingdom, which was to be a heavenly kingdom in the world.

Before ever our Lord set to work, John the Baptist was busy preparing a public for him; and his theme was: "The kingdom of heaven is at hand." When the Saviour began his public life, did he not constantly repeat those very words? (Matt. 4.17). "I must preach the gospel of God's kingdom . . .; it is for this that I was sent" (Luke 4.43). It was the good news of this kingdom that the Twelve were sent to make known. The six weeks of his risen appearances were spent in "telling them about the kingdom of God" (Acts. 1.3).

This kingdom is "within you": God's reign in souls. But it is visibly embodied in an external society on earth, entry into which can be obtained through faith and baptism. It has its charter, proclaimed in the sermon on the mount. The parables describing it show the presence of sinners and of scandals in it. It is to grow, slowly, as the seed grows into a bush, or leaven works throughout the lump of dough. Many citizens of the former kingdom will fail to gain membership of the new; whilst heathens "from the East and the West" will secure places in it. The kingdom has arrived, yet it has still to come, and we are to pray daily for its coming, for it is as yet only in its earthly phase; its final phase will come only after the end of time.

During our Lord's public ministry, his chief preoccupation was the training of the twelve men who were to be the pillars of his Kingdom; who had the right of admitting members, the office of teaching, of controlling and legislating, of selecting those who were to renew the offering of the great sacrifice: and at the head of all, the bearer of the keys of the kingdom, the Good Shepherd's deputy in charge of the flock. And the gates of hell should never prevail against it.

So, as the first Israel made its way through the desert towards the land of promise, under the leadership of Yahweh's representatives, so the new Israel marches through history towards the real promised land of heaven, led by divinely appointed leaders in the person of Peter and his successors.

The Catholic Church, in God's mind from eternity, is the perfect fulfilment of his promises—for the promises and prophecies, the types and figures of the old law are fulfilled in her, or they are not fulfilled at all. "Thou art my servant . . . thou art the Israel I claim for my own. . . . I have appointed thee to be the light of the Gentiles, in thee I will send out my salvation to the furthest corners of the earth" (Is. 49.3, 6), God had said to the first Israel—and that promise becomes a reality with the new Israel.

Such is the *kerygma,* the heralding of the good news of God's continuous interventions in favour of his people, the offer of community of love and life between him and his creatures, brought about in Christ.

Through all sacred history runs this unity of the divine plan.

Contemporary man is searching to discover a meaning in history. Marxism offers him a meaning. Yet there are not two histories, one sacred, the other secular: history is one, and it is the story of the divine purpose working itself out. Marx rightly taught us that history is dialectical. But not merely materialistic: on the contrary, it is a "spiritual dialectic, a dialogue between God and man" (Christopher Dawson). The process of history is made clear in the kerygmatic explanation of Catholicism, and it is this that must be given to the man of today.

The severe emphasis on the institutional aspect of the Church, imposed on us by post-Reformation controversial needs, can safely, in the world of today, relax somewhat and let the picture be completed by the more vital, immanent aspects. To see the first great intervention of God in the calling of Abraham; to understand the great steps of the historic process which prepared for man's redemption by Jesus Christ and the prolongation and application of his mission in the mystical Christ; to watch the new People of God on the march through history, transforming the world, moulding family and social life in the sense willed by God; to look forward to the parousia and to our Master's second coming in glory: all these considerations can fill the Catholic of today with joy, with hope, with dynamism. Each can see the importance of the gift of his baptism—of his calling by God, who so long ago called Abraham and

Moses and David and Jeremias and the Apostles; who now calls each of us to an irreplaceable apostolate in his particular conditions of life: to play his own part, however insignificant it may appear, in the vast historical development which leads from Abraham down to *me,* and forward thence to the end of time and to the hour when God will be all in all.

All this was implicitly foretold by one of Isaias' followers, who wrote, in words the Church proclaims for our meditation each Epiphany day: "Rise up, Jerusalem, and shine forth; thy dawn has come, and the glory of the Lord has broken upon thee. Darkness may envelop the earth, and all the nations lie in gloom; but upon thee the Lord shall dawn, over thee his splendour shall be revealed. Those rays of thine shall light the Gentiles on their path; kings shall walk in the splendour of thy sunrise. Lift up thy eyes and look about thee; who are all these that come flocking to thee? Sons of thine, daughters of thine, these shall come from far away, or rising up close at hand. How thy heart will overflow with wonder and gratitude at the sight, this multitude from over the sea, the wealth of the Gentiles pouring into thee . . . bringing . . . their cry of praise to the Lord" (Is. 60.1–6).

THE PLAN OF GOD

New Jerusalem, new Israel, God's flock, God's People, God's kingdom, spouse of Christ, body of Christ, Mother of men, the Catholic Church—God's purpose in creation.

The Tool of God

CHAPTER III

The Tool of God

INTRODUCTION

1. The scope of this paper is deliberately restricted in order to serve the purpose of the book as a whole. I am not writing about *our* Lady, I mean the Mary we know so well from our Catholic teaching and from our warm, personal experience; but about the Lady whom every careful reader of the Scriptures may come to know. The distinction is important. It may be helpful to enlarge upon it.

2. The history of heresy has proved that Mary is the good housewife of theology: she clears away the cobwebs in the house of God. In the fifth century her title Theotokos secured for ever a right faith in the manhood of the eternal Son; in the

twentieth, here in England, she provoked a clear and most helpful statement from our non-Catholic neighbours. In 1950, the impending definition of the dogma of her Assumption drew the following declaration from the Archbishops of Canterbury and of York:

> There is not the smallest evidence in the Scriptures or in the teaching of the early Church of belief in the doctrine of Mary's bodily assumption. The Church of England refuses to regard as requisite for saving faith any doctrine or opinions which are not plainly contained in the Scriptures.

Now here is a straightforward assertion and the Catholic welcomes it, though he disagrees profoundly since it contains the word "plainly." He welcomes it because unity is never achieved or sustained by misunderstanding. What is the Catholic view? That doctrines not plainly contained in the Scriptures may become plain, and requisite for saving faith, by the operation of the Spirit progressively enlightening the one true Church. Of these the Mary doctrine is a notable example,

74

and that is why it is so distinctively Catholic: for its complete acceptance it demands Catholic submission, for its full appreciation it needs Catholic devotion. For this same reason, it seems to me, the fullness of Mary doctrine is not apt material for exposition to the unsympathetic. But if people are Scripturally sympathetic, then we have a right and a recurring duty to present Mary to them as she is sketched in the Scriptures, hoping that they will come to the finished portrait in the end. Since for so many Mary means Rome and Rome is anathema, it must surely be sound policy to show that Mary means Scripture and that her outline is not so stubbornly Roman after all. And so this paper claims to give no more than a sketch of Mary, enough to show that the Catholic portrait is no caricature.

3. We have spoken of development in the Church's doctrine; it is hardly necessary to remind you that it is a feature of the Bible itself. The word of God spoke in various ways through the prophets and lastly by the Son. God speaks through both Old Testament and New and it is for us to heed the whole of his message. Nevertheless, it would be a great mistake to conceive the

Bible as one huge monolith, inflexible and homogeneous throughout. All is indeed the word of God, but God whispers or he cries aloud, according to the capacity of his hearers. And so when time's fullness comes, this same word can take to itself flesh, for the world to hear it from human lips. When God himself thus translates it, the poor efforts of the prophets are infinitely surpassed. What, then, are the prophets? The preparation for the mind of Christ. In the Old Testament therefore we shall look in vain, for instance, for the doctrine of the Trinity—which would indeed have been a threat at that period to the pure monotheism of Israel. But this does not mean to say that Israel's mind was not being prepared for it. Thus in Genesis the spirit of God moves over the waters as if it were the creative God himself, and yet in some sort his envoy also; thus also in the later doctrinal books the Word or Wisdom of God seems to assume, if only in poetic form, the dignity of a person. If we must be satisfied with these muttered hints of the Word himself, dare we expect anything at all for the Mother of the Word? Is there any suggestion at all of her in the Old Testament?

This paper seems to be full of cautions, and here is another. It too has its connection with the relationship of Scripture and Tradition of which we have spoken. The Synoptic Gospels and the Acts are an account of the *gesta Dei,* God's initiative for man, not man's for God. The accent is on action—God's action—not on human co-operation, still less on human virtues. In the course of centuries the Church has had time to sit back and admire the human actors in the drama, her communion of saints. The emphasis has changed, not illegitimately, from acting to being. Even the analysis of the nature of the Word incarnate is a shift of emphasis from the work of that Word. The Mary doctrine is part of the same movement.

The gospel stress is upon Mary the tool of God in his messianic plan—an apt tool indeed but a tool, one who is admired, but not so much for her own gifts as for the work she is chosen to do. For example: "He has regarded the humility of his handmaid" we translate our Lady's words. But she herself is not calling attention to a Christian virtue—the word itself is not humility as we understand it but simply lowly condition, insignificance. So also in the description of the Annunciation, which we shall have to examine, we all too readily translate: "Full of grace," as if the angel were paying her a compliment instead of declar-

77

ing a function. In fact the famous *kecharitomene* might be better translated: "highly privileged," i.e. to be the mother of the Messias—and "the Lord is with thee" is equally a promise of messianic triumph, not an idle greeting like "the Lord *be* with thee," nor a delicate salutation on Gabriel's part. This is how the gospels see Mary, and this explains our Lord's words to the woman: "Yea rather, blessed are they that hear the word of God and keep it."

OUR LADY IN THE OLD TESTAMENT

1. We may pass over a fact that may or not be considered curious, that though the father of the expected redeemer is never mentioned in the Old Testament, his mother is mentioned more than once. We had rather call attention to the strangely prominent part, especially strange in the Semitic world, played by a woman in the story not only of man's first fall but of the promise of his ultimate recovery. It is still more strange that the coming struggle is promised between the power of evil and Eve, not Adam: "I will set enmity between

thee *and the woman*." Adam is left in the background throughout and the future conqueror of the power of evil is described as the seed not of Adam but of the woman. I have warned you not to expect the clarity of the New Testament in the Old, still less the clarity of our God-guided tradition in either, but this at least must be said: that given the undoubted close historical association of Jesus and his mother, the mist moves away from the ancient text. The Fathers were quick to notice it and they found a satisfying fitness in this, that when the time came for the primeval curse to be reversed, the old order of things was reversed also, and it was not Eve who was drawn from the side of Adam but the second Adam drawn from a virgin by God's creative hand; that the curse of the fruit of the tree became "blessed is the fruit of thy womb."

2. But this notion of a new, a second, Eve, does not stand thus isolated in the Biblical tradition. We might almost say that in the framework of Biblical thought it is all but inevitable. I would remind you that when the prophets painted the picture of the future golden age for which they longed, they dipped their brush in the colours of the garden of Eden. It was not, indeed, that they

hoped for a return and no more. The Greeks with their cyclic idea of time might so have hoped, and did in fact. But the prophets were Semites: the firm conviction of a driving Providence made them see time as a straight and ascending line travelling surely to a higher goal. For the prophets, each event of Israel's history was at once a presage and a guarantee of even better things to come. There is not time to vindicate this principle, which in truth needs no vindication, for it is accepted by all. When therefore the prophet Isaias declares in the name of God: "I will make Sion's desert like an Eden" (51.3), it is not Paradise Regained he thinks of, but a new Paradise bettered beyond imagining. The garden, then, is to flourish again in unearthly beauty. What of its inhabitants? Are they to return, too? In the Jewish, as in the Christian, tradition, two of them most certainly reappear. In the first place Adam: the prophet Daniel calls the future redeemer a "son of man," which is in Hebrew "son of Adam"; our Lord makes the title peculiarly his own, and St. Paul is not slow to take the hint: "The first man was of the earth, earthly; the second man from heaven, heavenly" (1 Cor. 15.47). The serpent, too, puts in his appearance to trouble the peace of God's people.

The prophet Isaias presents the godless enemy under that figure and in the gospel of John the serpent, the liar from the beginning, is the one enemy of the redeemer; in the Apocalypse also the dragon, the primeval serpent, attacks the mysterious Woman and her child only to be finally cast down to the bottomless pit. The garden is to return, then, and Adam and the serpent. What has become of Eve? Has she no place in the great victory as she had such a prominent place in the defeat and in the promise of triumph? It is difficult to think so. There are in fact indications to the contrary.

3. There is a passage in the prophecies of Isaias which recalls the old idyll of Eden where the beasts are the friend of man and the lion and the lamb are at peace together, where a child eats butter and honey as in the golden age. Within this very passage the prophet announces the maiden who is to conceive and bring forth a son whose name is "God-With-Us." Of this word "maiden" there has been much discussion. We shall say nothing of it except that the idea of divine intervention in the birth of chosen children was an idea familiar to Israel from the birth of Isaac to the birth of Samuel; we should also observe that over one

hundred years before our Lord's coming the Jewish translators of Isaias into Greek chose the unequivocal word *parthenos,* virgin, to render it. But perhaps not enough attention has been called to another tiny word (it is only a letter in Hebrew), the definite article: Behold *the* maiden shall conceive. The prophet surely invites his contemporaries to recognize some maiden already well known to them from a literary tradition almost lost to us, an ideal figure familiar to his audience. To reinforce this impression come the words of Micheas, contemporary of Isaias: "Thou Bethlehem, out of thee shall come forth unto me he that is to be ruler in Israel; whose origin is of old, of ancient days. Therefore will he give them up until the time when she who is to bring forth brings forth; then the remnant of his brethren shall return to the children of Israel." Both prophets would seem to take it for granted that this mysterious woman is well known—even expected.

Where in the Biblical tradition is there such a one? Is it not the old story of Eden that comes most naturally to mind? May it not be that if the garden and the serpent and Adam are in some sense to come again, so is Eve? Is it fanciful to suggest that whereas the effect of the first sin was to subject woman to man, the first sign of the lifting of the curse was a virgin-birth in which man had no part? It is even possible that in the prophecy of Micheas, the "old, the ancient days" refer back to the origin of our race, to Adam, and that the one who is to bring forth refers back to Eve, of whom it was written in Genesis that she was to bring forth in sorrow. The very early and stubborn Eve-symbolism in the Fathers needs some explanation, and perhaps we have it here.

OUR LADY IN THE NEW TESTAMENT

1. But these are the shadows of the old Testament and perhaps I have shown only that they are shadows. Let us turn to the substance of the New. We shall not mention the gospel of St. Mark, since he omits the account of our Lord's birth and childhood and has nothing to say of our Lady in addition to what we have from the other gospels. Nor shall we delay over Matthew who, after all, writes of the Infancy of Jesus from Joseph's point of view; Mary is so passive throughout. There is no angelic annunciation to her but only an explana-

tion to Joseph, and it is Joseph who takes the young mother to Egypt and back to Nazareth again. We pause merely to mention Matthew's precious little phrase, four times used and so pointedly, "the child and his mother." These two, thus isolated from Joseph, are nevertheless Joseph's responsibility: "Arise, take the child and his mother and take flight into Egypt"—which gives us a poignant impression at once of their helplessness and of their value beyond price.

2. Since the Epistles and, in all probability, the Apocalypse have nothing directly to say, we find ourselves left with the gospels of Luke and of John. Now first a word about these two evangelists. Modern scholars are beginning to notice that they have much in common that is not to be found in Matthew or Mark. To the list of these topics we must add their interest in Mary. It has been conjectured, perhaps rather rashly, that the two met in Rome twenty or thirty years after the Ascension. If so, the beloved disciple who took Mary as his own would have much to tell Luke. But however this may be, their gospels must have met at some period of their composition, and one result is the enthusiasm for Mary which you find in both.

3. Let us take Luke first: Luke, who in his first two chapters lays the foundation, the only sure foundation, of Mary's dignity, which is her divine motherhood; Luke, who as "the scribe of the gentleness of Christ" was peculiarly fitted to be the evangelist of the gentle mother. At the beginning of his gospel Luke tells us that he has "ascertained all things carefully from the beginning," and then immediately deserts his elegant Greek opening to plunge into a Semitic style unnatural to him. Leaving aside the problem of an edition or successive editions of his source of information, there is no doubt that it comes from a Hebrew mind. Indeed a severe critic like Harnack ventured to say "Mary's mind," and in effect the very intimacy of the information is almost enough to prove it. The evangelist himself seems to invite us to the same conclusion when on two separate occasions, once after the shepherd's visit, the second time after the finding in the Temple, he goes out of his way to notice that Mary "kept all these words in her heart." How did he know but ultimately from Mary? And what else did Mary tell him?

4. There is an interesting device which attentive readers have observed in Luke's first two

chapters. In describing the origin and birth of the Baptist and of Jesus he constructs the accounts in parallel: of each child is described the annunciation by Gabriel, the birth, circumcision, imposition of name. And lest we miss his purpose Luke concludes each account in almost the same words. For the Baptist: "And the child grew and was strengthened in spirit." For our Lord: "And Jesus advanced in wisdom and age and grace with God and men." This quite deliberate comparison is instructive provided we remember that it is also a contrast designed to bring out the higher dignity of the one whom the Baptist in his later days was to declare "greater than I." With this in mind we may compare Luke's story of the two annunciations. The contrast with Mary's annunciation is striking: Zachary's had been in the pomp of the Jerusalem Temple, Mary's is in the little-known hamlet of Nazareth. Of Zachary Luke says that he was frightened when he saw the angel, but he notes no fear in Mary. But the climax of Luke's comparison lies in the contrasting conception of the children. Of old, God had pursued his favours to Israel by miraculous intervention: so Isaac had been born to the aging Sara, so Samuel to Anna. Now in the new dispensation we see the work of the same divine hand. To Zachary it is said that a child, not the less his own child, shall be born to his aging wife. But what to Mary? There must be some greater sign here—the contrast demands it and the text asserts it: "How shall this be done?" asks the virgin, "because I know not man." And Gabriel answers: "The Holy Ghost shall come upon thee and the power of the most High shall overshadow thee." The birth of Isaac, the birth of Samuel, the birth of the Baptist are nothing to this. This time it is a virgin who conceives and brings forth a son.

We might add here, though rather *en passant*, that this parallel method of Luke's has something useful to say on the textual side as well as on that of interpretation. Whatever doubts may be thrown on the Baptist-Jesus parallel as a whole, and they do not to us appear grave, there is no mistaking the diptych of the two annunciations themselves:

Fear not, Zachary	Fear not, Mary
Your wife shall bear a son	You shall bear a son
He shall be great before the Lord	He shall be great and called Son of the Most High

Now in the first panel of the diptych Zachary follows up with a question, asking a sign: "How shall I know this?" It would be rather strange if Mary in the second panel did not ask a question, too; and so in fact our text makes her say: "How shall this be?" One has surely the right to oppose this internal textual argument to Harnack's more subjective and equally internal argument against the primitive character of this verse and its following.

5. We have deliberately understated the Old Testament case for Mary though many think it strong. For my part I think that such an argument at least does away with the surprise that others may feel at the prominence of a woman in the scheme of salvation, and to that extent prepares the way for Mary. Let us leave it at that. But this does not mean that the Old Testament has no place at all in this matter. The annunciation to Zachary is full of Old Testament reference: the same Gabriel who appeared to Daniel at the time of evening sacrifice appears to Zachary in the hour of incense; to Daniel he announced the coming of a holy of holies, to Zachary the coming of a holy child; like Samuel, miracle son of the barren Anna, the child of the aging Elizabeth, he is *nazir*—con-

secrated to God by abstention from wine; Samson's mother, previously sterile, abstained also, and thus consecrated her unborn son. Of Samson in the book of Judges, of Samuel in the first book of Kings, of the Baptist in Luke it is said that "the child grew up before the Lord." It looks as if Luke was trying to show how the Baptist was the heir to the central figures of Israel's history: Samuel, Samson and explicitly Elias.

6. Taking this broad hint from Luke we may now see what the Old Testament has to do with the annunciation to Mary. There is one word in particular whose Biblical overtones have been until recently overlooked. I mean the word "overshadow"—"the power of the Most High shall overshadow thee." The inspired writers wrote so frequently with an eye upon the work of their predecessors that, in time, certain phrases became technical and cannot be fully understood unless their history is known. Now the word "overshadow," sufficiently unusual to show that Luke uses it very deliberately, has its history. In the ancient Greek translation of the Old Testament it is used frequently to express the coming of the bright cloud which the Rabbis called the "sheki-

nah" or "dwelling," which is defined as the majestic presence or manifestation of God descending to dwell with men. This shekinah is also called the *kabod* or *doxa* or "glory."

And indeed this dwelling of God with men is the dream of the Old Testament. It had its origin at the time of the Exodus from Egypt when Israel was still a quasi-nomad race. When God wished to assure Israel of his presence he commanded Moses to make a tent, a tabernacle, for his dwelling. This tent was pitched in the midst of Israel's encampment: no nation had its gods so near. And when the tent was pitched, says the book of Exodus, "a cloud covered the tent and the glory of the Lord filled the tabernacle and Moses was not able to enter because the cloud *overshadowed* it." It is the word Luke uses. This overshadowing is therefore intimately connected with the idea of divine dwelling, of the presence of God. In the same way the overshadowing glory-cloud is said to hover over the Ark of the Covenant between the sculptured figures of the cherubim—hence the expression "who sittest upon the cherubim." This ancient idea of the glory-cloud of God's presence persists through the prophets; when Zacharias, for example, speaks of the glorious future, he uses the

words of God: "Rejoice, daughter of Sion, for I am
coming to pitch my tent among you." So too in the
later Jewish tradition noted in the second book of
Machabees (2.5ff.) both tabernacle and Ark were
expected to reappear when the kingdom of God
should be re-established.

Here we may pause for a moment to call attention to a link between the text of Zacharias and
that of Luke, a passage from Sophonias (3.14–
17). Here it is, side by side with Luke's text:

Rejoice, daughter of Sion	Rejoice (not "hail") full of grace
Yahweh is in thee (lit. "in thy womb")	The Lord is with thee
Fear not, Sion	Fear not, Mary
Thy God is in thee (lit. "in thy womb")	Thou shalt conceive in thy womb
A mighty Saviour	Thou shalt call his name Saviour

It is difficult to think that Luke is not seeing in
Mary at this moment the counterpart of the hill
of Sion, the place of the Temple.

We are now in a position to understand the

words in which the gospel of John describes the Incarnation: "The Word became flesh and set up his tent among us and we saw his glory." But we have observed that John has much in common with Luke; here in Gabriel's words reported by Luke we have precisely John's picture of the overshadowing glory-cloud, sign of the Presence. Until the birth of the child the home of the Presence is Mary's bosom. She is the tabernacle of the new covenant, the tent of God's new dwelling with men. She is the God-bearing Ark. This, I think, is certainly what Luke meant to imply.

What follows is somewhat more conjectural and coincidence may account for it, but it is at least interesting that Luke's account of the Visitation suggests that Elizabeth recognized in Mary the new Ark of the Covenant: her words come oddly near King David's cry of humility: "How shall the Ark of the Lord come to me?" when she exclaims: "Whence is this that the Mother of my Lord should come to me?" We might go even further and remind ourselves that as David is said to have "skipped" before the Ark of the Lord for very joy, so the unborn Baptist "skips" (an unusual word) in the womb at Mary's presence. And just as it is written that David left the Ark in the house of Obededom for three months and its presence blessed the whole household, so Mary the new Ark remained in Zachary's house for three months.

7. It is time now to turn to John—to John who took Mary to his home or, according to another possible rendering, took her as a legacy. There are two, only two, incidents that lift the veil from Mary. The first is Cana, the second the Cross. The events are well known and I shall be content with one or two remarks.

There is a Semitic literary device, commonly called "inclusion"; one single phrase or idea is used twice, once at the beginning and once at the end, in order to sandwich a passage. John himself adopts it: thus his Prologue declares "in him was life" and the true finale of his gospel is "that believing you may have life in his name." So also in the same gospel our Lord is first hailed as the lamb of God and when all is over the text of the paschal lamb is applied to him: "You shall not break a bone." This literary method serves to illumine by its forward and backward glance the outline of the matter between. "What I said at the beginning," it seems to say, "I invite you to consider again and not forget." Now this phenomenon

occurs precisely in the two Mary passages of the
fourth gospel—Cana and the Cross; they are
pendants one of another: in each case the mother
of Jesus was there, in each case she is addressed as
"woman," on the first occasion there was water
and wine, on the second water and blood; Cana is
called the "beginning of miracles when he first
manifested his glory," the Cross—in John's gospel
—is the climax of glory, Our Lord's "lifting up"—
and the evangelist says carefully that when Jesus
had said "Behold thy Mother" he knew that all
things were accomplished. Mary was there at the
beginning and there at the end; indeed she provoked the beginning and sealed the end. Could the
evangelist have said more clearly what importance
he attached to her?

8. The second remark is this. John is not in the
habit of reporting incidents for the satisfaction of
historical curiosity only. Throughout his gospel,
which the Fathers call the spiritual gospel, he is
profoundly theological—he is concerned with the
deeper significance of things (why else did he call
its hero the Word?). Contrast if you will the iden-
tical miracle of the loaves as described by the first
three gospels with John's account which is fol-

lowed, as in the other three it is not, by the profound theology of the Bread of Life discourse. Compare Luke's raising of the widow's son, that lovely but brief account, with John's raising of Lazarus which is followed by the long sermon on Christ the Resurrection and the Life.

Now even in his account of the Crucifixion John narrates nothing that has no further point than its purely historical value—no details are given that are not deliberately pointed by some reference to the Old Testament. Even that one which seems an exception—I mean the seamless garment—suggests the priesthood of Christ, since the high priest's robe was without seam. It follows surely that we must approach the interpretation of our Lord's words to his mother from the Cross in a thoughtful spirit, seeking a deeper level. It is not only that John had his duty to Mary: "Behold thy mother," but that Mary had something to do for him: "Woman, behold thy son." Did John need mothering in the ordinary sense? If so, his own mother stood by the Cross too. In the whole context that I have hinted at, it is therefore not improbable that this text will bear the weight that so many Catholics put upon it. Nevertheless, it is well to be warned that the doctrine of Mary's universal motherhood does not rest on any single text: it is rooted deep in the Scriptural theology of Redemption and of Grace, as the great Origen pointed out eighteen hundred years ago. John's gospel had retained the saying: "I in them and thou in me"; St. Paul cried: "I live now not I but Christ lives in me." Now, says Origen, "since the Christian himself lives no longer but Christ lives in him, the words apply to him that were spoken to Mary: Behold thy son."

CONCLUSION

Mary is honoured because she is the mother of the king: "Whence is this that the mother of my lord the king should come to me?" In the palace of Solomon the queen mother's throne stood side by side with the king's and Bathsheba had great influence with her son, as Balthasar's mother had with him in the book of Daniel. The post-Reformation Western world might profess itself horrified at the Queen-Mother's privileged position; I am sure the early Christian would not.